Text and illustrations © Reverend Liz England 2023

Bibleadventuresteddyanddolly@gmail.com

Published by Dancing Waves Books

ISBN 978-1-7392421-0-7

First published 2023

All rights reserved

The author asserts the moral right to be identified as the author of this work

Bible Adventures

Teddy and Dolly and the Great Storm	3
Teddy and the Picnic	7
Teddy the Samaritan	11
Teddy and Dolly Clean the House	15
Dolly the Shepherd	21
Teddy and the Lost Coin	25
Dolly and her Dad	29
Teddy Climbs a Tree	35
How to use these stories	39
Where are these Bible stories?	41

Teddy and Dolly and the Great Storm

This was the biggest, darkest, loudest storm they'd ever seen. This storm had the biggest clouds, the darkest skies, the loudest bangs, the flashiest flashes and the wettest rain. Can you imagine?

Do you remember a loud storm?
I would cover my ears.
Can you cover your ears?

Well, Teddy and Dolly were in a boat with their friends, and the lake they were on was the worst place they could be during a storm.

Teddy looked at the dark clouds and then looked at his knees, they were shaking – he was scared. Can you shake your knees?

Dolly looked at the large waves crashing onto their small boat and held on even tighter to the side. She felt a bit queasy in her tummy.

Teddy looked around at the frightened and worried faces of his friends and made a decision. 'Right,' he said, 'we are waking Jesus up!' You see, Jesus was on the boat, and not only that, he was asleep. And Jesus was still asleep despite the noise, the rain and the waves.

Dolly nodded and they ran together to Jesus. Kneeling down next to his sleeping figure they gently woke him. 'Master, save us! We're going to drown,' said Dolly. 'Don't you care?' said Teddy.

Jesus woke and looked at the storm, then looked at Teddy and Dolly. 'Why are you so frightened? Why are you so afraid?
Did you not remember I was here with you?'

And then Jesus did something even more amazing – Jesus stood up, raised his hand and spoke to the wind as if the wind was his friend. 'Silence, wind!' Then Jesus spoke to the sea – 'Quieten down, sea.'

Then Jesus spoke to the storm – 'Silence, storm!'

And do you know what?

The wind, the sea and the storm did exactly that, they did exactly what Jesus had told them to do. The wind stopped, the sea became smooth, with not even a ripple, and the sun came out. All was calm.

Can you imagine?

Teddy and Dolly rubbed their eyes, astounded with what they'd seen happen right in front of them. Dolly turned to Teddy and whispered,
'Wow, even the wind and the waves listen to him.'

Teddy and the Picnic

Teddy made himself a picnic. He had planned to go and hear Jesus speak, as apparently Jesus was going to be visiting the town that day. Hooray!

When Teddy got to the place where Jesus was there was a huge crowd – at least 5,000 people all wanting to hear what Jesus was saying.

Teddy held on to his lunch carefully as he did not want to drop it or lose it in this big crowd. Teddy found somewhere to sit down and rest his legs near the front and started to listen.

Jesus spoke about love and forgiveness and other wonderful exciting things.

Teddy's tummy rumbled – I am hungry, he thought and started to think about the bread and fish he had in his lunch bag.

One of Jesus' friends whispered something to Jesus. It sounded like he was suggesting the crowd go somewhere else for lunch, maybe to a nearby town.

Then Jesus did an amazing thing. He started to look at Teddy. Teddy looked back at Jesus. Jesus said, 'Teddy, would you mind sharing your lunch with everyone?'

Teddy looked surprised. 'But Jesus,' Teddy said. 'I only have five bread rolls and two fish – not enough for all of these people!' Jesus' friends nodded in agreement.

'But...' Teddy said. 'I would be happy to share.' Hooray!

So, Jesus took Teddy's lunch and told his friends to get the crowd to sit in groups. Jesus took the five bread rolls and two fish, looked up to heaven and said a thank you prayer. Then he broke the loaves and gave them to his twelve friends to give to the crowd.

And do you know what? Everybody there, including Teddy ate enough yummy food and their tummies were happy and full! Hooray!

And amazingly the food that was left over was picked up and filled 12 baskets!!

Teddy the Samaritan

Teddy and Dolly were out for a walk one day, when up ahead they saw a group of people being unkind to a boy. The boy was very hurt and fell to the floor. Teddy and Dolly saw the group run away.

But suddenly a businessman appeared around the corner. Teddy and Dolly were glad when they saw the man on his way to the boy.
He will help!

Teddy and Dolly watched as the businessman took one look at the poorly boy and then looked at his watch and ran off in the opposite direction. He obviously had something more important to do.

They then saw a doctor approaching.
She will help!

Unfortunately, the doctor pretended to not see the boy and hurried past also. Dolly said, 'Teddy, we'd better go and see how the boy is doing,'

and Dolly ran up the road to where the boy was lying.
Dolly will help!

Teddy watched and saw Dolly turn her face away. Dolly said loudly so Teddy could hear it clearly, 'Ergghh - he is really dirty and smells bad, as well as having cuts and bruises on him - I can't possibly help him. Somebody else should.' Dolly then ran home, as quickly as she could, to wash her hands.

After Dolly had run off Teddy walked up to the poorly boy. Teddy could tell that the boy was hurt and needed help so Teddy spoke gently to the boy to reassure him. Teddy then bathed his wounds and stuck some plasters on the sore bits. Teddy then gently lifted the boy and carried him to the nearest café, bought him a burger and left some money so the boy could have some pudding.

Later, when Dolly heard the story of how Teddy had helped the boy, she was proud of Teddy as he had shown such kindness. She was also sad that she hadn't helped the boy when she could have.

Teddy and Dolly went to visit the boy at his home later that day and took him some flowers and chocolates to help him get better quickly.

Teddy and Dolly Clean the House

Once upon a time there was a teddy and a dolly and they were best friends. They lived together in a house with a red roof and a yellow door. Every day Teddy decided that they needed to clean the house, and today was no different. Teddy decided that as the windows had only been cleaned seven hours ago, they needed cleaning again and Teddy decided that as the floor had only been mopped five hours ago it needed mopping again.

Teddy called, 'Dolly, Dolly, come and help me clean.' Dolly ran towards Teddy and started to get on with the cleaning. They cleaned together, they mopped together and they polished together. Then the doorbell rang (Ding-Dong). Dolly ran to the door and opened it wide.
It was Justin Bieber who happened to be popping by.
'Hello,' he said. 'Can I come in for a drink?'

'Hello,' said Dolly and she was just about to invite him in when Teddy came to see who it was.

Teddy took one look at Justin and then one cross look at Dolly and slammed the door closed.

'We have important work to do,' Teddy said.

'We have got no time for people.'

Dolly was sad.

Dolly and Teddy carried on with the polishing and the hoovering until the doorbell rang again (Ding-Dong). Dolly ran to the door and opened it wide. It was the Queen of England and she took her crown off as she said, 'Please could I come in and sit for a while?'

Dolly opened the door wider and smiled at the queen.

'Of course, your majesty, do come in,' she said.

Teddy saw what was happening and quickly turned the queen around and ushered her back out of the door.

Dolly asked, 'Teddy why can't we talk to people?'
'Because we haven't got time – there is too much work to do,' Teddy said. And that was that for the time being.

Dolly scrubbed the bathroom, and Teddy cleaned the shoes and dusted the mirrors. They were feeling very tired when the doorbell rang for the third time (Ding-Dong).
Teddy frowned as Dolly slowly opened the door.

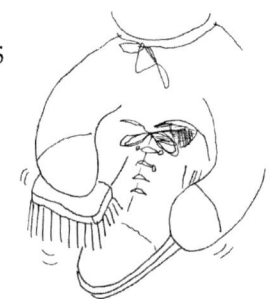

Jesus walked in and sat down on one of their shiny chairs.

Dolly said, 'Welcome Jesus, it is great to see you,' and Dolly sat down at Jesus' feet. Jesus and Dolly talked together for a long time.

After a while Teddy had had enough and came to stand right in front of Jesus. Teddy said, 'Jesus, don't you care that Dolly has left me to do all of the work by myself? Tell her to come and help me.'

Jesus said, 'Teddy, Teddy, you are so worried about all these things. Dolly has chosen the right thing and it will not be taken away from her.'

Teddy was so surprised and thought that what Jesus had said was so clever that he sat at Jesus' feet and listened too.

And do you know what? After Jesus had gone Teddy and Dolly felt a lot better, and from then on always invited people to come in whenever possible, just in case Jesus decided to come back.

Dolly the Shepherd

Dolly the Shepherd had 100 sheep. She would count them each night to make sure they were all safely in their pens.

Teddy once asked Dolly if her sheep had any names and Teddy was surprised when Dolly told him she knew all of their names.

That one is Woolly, that one is fuzzy, that one is Bernard and that one is Marigold – she went on until Teddy had heard all of the 100 sheep's names! Phew! What a lot of sheep!

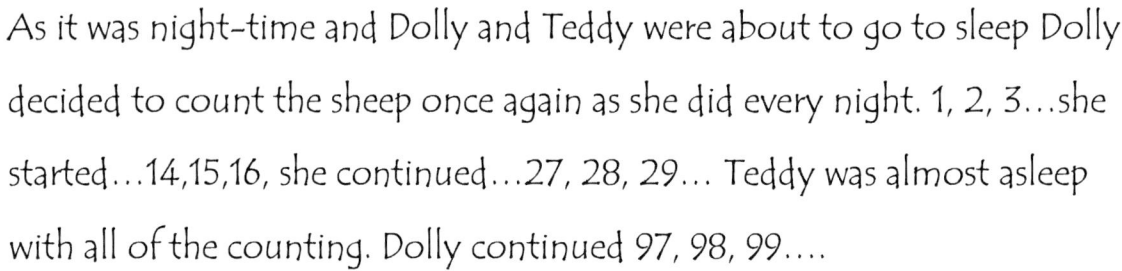

As it was night-time and Dolly and Teddy were about to go to sleep Dolly decided to count the sheep once again as she did every night. 1, 2, 3…she started…14,15,16, she continued…27, 28, 29… Teddy was almost asleep with all of the counting. Dolly continued 97, 98, 99….

WHAT! One of the sheep was missing!

Teddy looked at Dolly's shocked face (can you all do a shocked face?) and asked her what she was going to do?

And Dolly said,
'I am going to find my lost sheep!'
And off she went, over hills,
along muddy paths - squelch, squelch, squelch!
through dark forests with lots of tall trees - whoooooo!
across fields with swishy grass - swish, swish, swish!
until finally in a prickly hedge she found her sheep.
'Woolly,' she exclaimed as she picked up the sheep
and cuddled him.

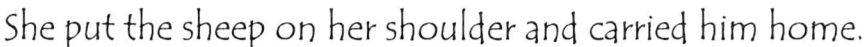

She put the sheep on her shoulder and carried him home.
Across the fields with swishy grass - swish, swish, swish!
through the forest with tall trees - whoooooo!

along the muddy path – squelch, squelch, squelch!
back over the hill, until Dolly and Woolly were safely back home.

And do you know what? Dolly was so happy to have found the lost sheep that she invited Teddy over to have a party with her.

'My sheep was lost and now he is found, let's celebrate,' Dolly said and Teddy and Dolly did just that by eating cake and drinking lemonade. (What else would you have eaten at the party?)

Teddy and the Lost Coin

Teddy had had a very long day! He was tired YAWN! But he had been working hard and earning money. Hooray! Teddy had carefully saved up his money and now had ten gold coins! Wowee! Look how shiny and bright they are.

Let's count the coins with teddy…
1,2,3,4,5,6,7,8,9,10

The coins were very special to Teddy and he kept them in a special box that had a lid with his name on.

One day Teddy counted the coins again…1,2,3,4,5,6,7,8,9…

Oh no, one of the coins was missing!

So, Teddy decided to look for it.

He looked under the bed,

he looked up high on a shelf,

he looked in the fridge…

he found a cream cake and ate a bit,

but there was no gold coin!

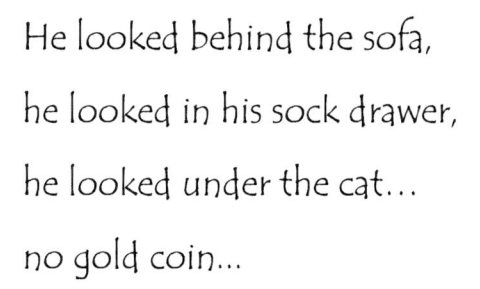

He looked behind the sofa,

he looked in his sock drawer,

he looked under the cat…

no gold coin…

then he thought a little bit… and swept the floor carefully…

chink, chink… he found the coin… hooray!

Teddy had found his lost coin and there were now ten again.

'I am so happy,' said Teddy, 'I am going to have a party.'

So, Teddy invited Dolly to the house. And Teddy invited some other friends and neighbours. Then they all had a party with strawberries and bananas, and of course some cream cake.

And that is the same as the party that happens in heaven when someone who doesn't know God starts to find out about him.

Dolly and her Dad

Dolly lived in a house with her dad and her brother.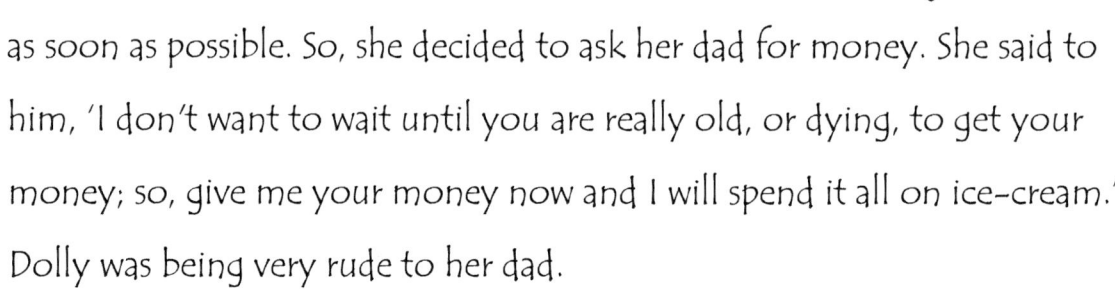
One day Dolly had some ice-cream, it was so delicious!
Dolly realised she wanted to eat lots and lots of ice-cream
as soon as possible. So, she decided to ask her dad for money. She said to him, 'I don't want to wait until you are really old, or dying, to get your money; so, give me your money now and I will spend it all on ice-cream.'
Dolly was being very rude to her dad.

Dolly's dad was sad, but, despite Dolly's rudeness, he gave her his money and hoped she would spend it wisely.

Well, Dolly left home with all the money and went to a big town far away. The town had shiny buildings and sparkly people, and Dolly was so happy she had come to this town. Dolly began to spend her money.

Dolly made a lot of friends who liked it when she spent money on them.

Dolly would buy her friends lots of things such as yummy food and beautiful clothes and she would invite them to travel around in a helicopter with her.

Dolly also ate lots of ice-cream
- strawberry, raspberry, caramel,
chocolate, fudge, chocolate fudge
and even marmite ice-cream.
She had ice-cream every day, for every meal.
Dolly soon started to feel sick in her tummy.

Dolly also ran out of money. Oh dear!

And as soon as Dolly had run out of money, do you know what happened? Her new friends did not want to be friends with her anymore.

All alone and sad Dolly didn't know what to do. She began to get hungry, but without money she couldn't buy any food.

Poor Dolly!

Dolly had to get a job and she eventually found one, feeding pigs to help a local farmer. Dolly didn't like pigs. The pigs were pink and smelly.
But Dolly was so hungry she almost ate some of the pig's food.

Dolly was very sad and very sorry.

She thought about her dad, and how rude she'd been. Dolly knew that if she said sorry to him, he might let her come home and work for him, perhaps as his cleaner, until the money she had spent was paid back.

At least as his cleaner she would get fed
– so she wouldn't be hungry anymore.

So, Dolly started to walk the long way back home.

But while she was still a long way away her dad saw her through his binoculars. Her dad had been waiting on a big hill for many weeks just in case Dolly came back.

Dad ran down the hill and along the path with a big smile on his face.

He then picked Dolly up in a big hug and swung her around giving her lots of kisses. Dolly was surprised and started to say sorry, and also Dolly loved being hugged by her dad.

But her dad was not waiting for a sorry, he instead got the best cloak and put it on her, and put the best jewellery on her head and neck, and gave her the best, comfiest shoes for her aching feet.

Also, he had planned a party. He had made some party hats and yummy food. Dad said, 'This daughter of mine was lost and now she has been found. We need to have a party and celebrate.' Hooray!

Teddy Climbs a Tree

Teddy was in a tree. He had climbed up a short while ago and was now balancing on a couple of branches. Why was Teddy in a tree, you may be wondering?

Because today he was trying to see Jesus who was visiting Jericho, where Teddy lived. And Teddy was quite short and the tall tree helped him to see more easily.

Teddy had also been greedy and sold his work for too much money, so he was escaping from other people in the gathered crowd who were still cross with him.

Teddy waited patiently for Jesus to arrive and tried not to fall out of the tree; he clung on to the branches tightly. And when Jesus did arrive, Jesus stood at the base of the tree and looked up at Teddy.

'Teddy,' Jesus called out. 'I want to have tea with you today; I want to come to your house and share some cake with you.'

Well, Teddy was amazed and couldn't believe his luck! He was overjoyed with the thought of eating with Jesus!

However, the other people in the crowd overheard Jesus' invitation to Teddy and they got cross and angry, and jealous. They called Teddy horrid names and questioned loudly why Jesus, who was such a good person, wanted to eat cake with this very bad Teddy.

But Teddy suddenly felt very sad that he had been so greedy and mean to the people and after thinking for a few moments shouted out saying, 'Jesus, I am sorry for cheating people and for being greedy and mean. I'll now give away half of all my money to people who have no money and if I am caught cheating again I'll pay four times the amount back.'

Jesus looked at the people and then smiled as he looked at Teddy. Jesus said, 'today is a very happy day, as this Teddy was lost and now he is found.'

How to use these stories

These stories are to be used individually, in one-to-ones or in any group or service that you can imagine! Tell them and repeat them anywhere. I always hope they will be rewarding to the reader and the listeners.

You will need a 'teddy' and a 'dolly' – size, colour, character doesn't matter; I've used knitted ones that church members have made for me, cardboard ones, drawn ones, ones from charity shops… If you are doing these stories regularly then I'd suggest you use the same Teddy and Dolly as I find children and adults get used to the characters.

I have also told these stories (at a baptism with 300 people) with a presentation using a screen. This worked well due to the size of the congregation.

There are sometimes other characters where other toys can be used. I have found that knitted eight inch toy dolls and teddies work the best.

These Teddy and Dolly adventures are best read out loud and as slowly as possible. Take your time. Pause for effect or for the more emotional parts as it will take a time for the audience to take in what is being said.

I have aimed to print the stories clearly so you can use them directly to tell each story.

Do let me know how you get on and which other stories you would find useful to be told in this way - Bibleadventuresteddyanddolly@gmail.com

Where are these Bible stories?

Teddy and Dolly and the Great Storm p.3   Matthew 8: 23-27
Mark 4: 35-41
Luke 8: 22-25

Teddy and the Picnic p.7   Matthew 14: 13-21
Mark 6: 30-44
Luke 9: 10-17
John 6: 1-14

Teddy the Samaritan p.11   Luke 10: 30-37

Teddy and Dolly Clean the House p.15   Luke 10: 38-42

Dolly the Shepherd p.21   Matthew 18: 10-12
Luke 15: 1-7

Teddy and the Lost Coin p.25   Luke 15: 8-10

Dolly and her Dad p.29   Luke 15: 11-32

Teddy Climbs a Tree p.35   Luke 19: 1-10

42